# FALLING AWAKE

# FALLING AWAKE

Poems by
Gary Margolis

THE UNIVERSITY OF GEORGIA PRESS
ATHENS AND LONDON

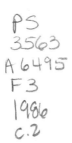

© 1986 by Gary Margolis
Published by the University of Georgia Press
Athens, Georgia 30602

Designed by Betty McDaniel
Set in 10 on 13 Linotron 202 Optima Medium

The paper in this book meets the guidelines for
permanence and durability of the Committee on
Production Guidelines for Book Longevity of the
Council on Library Resources.

Printed in the United States of America

90  89  88  87  86      5  4  3  2  1

Library of Congress Cataloging in Publication Data

Margolis, Gary.
    Falling awake.

    I. Title.
PS3563.A6495F3  1986    811'.54    85-16509
ISBN 0-8203-0825-0 (alk. paper)
ISBN 0-8203-0826-9 (pbk. : alk. paper)


The lines of Chateaubriand in the epigraph can be
found in Claude Levi-Strauss's *Tristes Tropiques*,
translated by John Russell, Hutchinson & Co.,
London, 1961, pp. 45–46.


The publication of this book is supported by a
grant from the National Endowment for the Arts,
a federal agency.

# ACKNOWLEDGMENTS

The author and publisher gratefully acknowledge the following publications in which poems from this volume first appeared, sometimes in earlier versions.

*The American Scholar:* "Beyond Resembling"
*The Antigonish Review:* "Using the Air"
*College English:* "It's Something," "Borne Away"
*Crazy Horse:* "Moon of Another Childhood"
*The Denver Quarterly:* "Pearl of the Moon," "Knock Back"
*The Louisville Review:* "The Way Out," "What to Forget,"
  "Positively Blue"
*North American Review:* "Waiting at the Office of Magritte"
*Poetry:* "Having Watched *The Day After*," "If You Asked,"
  "Away from Any Uniform"
*Poetry Northwest:* "Falling Awake"
*Prairie Schooner:* "Dancing at Bread Loaf," "Between Us,"
  "Inside"
*Tendril:* "Her Apprehension"

The author again wishes to express his gratitude to Edna Puls, friend and colleague; to Middlebury College;

and to Sam Dietzel, friend, counselor, fisherman.

IN MEMORY OF MY MOTHER
AND FOR MY FATHER

AND FOR SAM AND ARIANA

When they are older and can read
by themselves the name of this place,
they will have taken their first steps
away from us, who walked out of the sea,
carrying as many of them as we could hold.

# CONTENTS

IV

V

VI

Every man carries within himself
a world made up of all that he has
seen and loved; and it is to this
world that he returns, incessantly,
though he may pass through, and
seem to inhabit, a world quite
foreign to it.

—Chateaubriand, *Voyage en Italie*

I

# KNOCK BACK

The smallest of them, the downy,
learned to cling to a suet net
as if it were bark and pick at

the beef fat until spring returned
its store of eggs and grubs.
All through history, and thus

literature, men and women have been
cursed and blessed into trees
when they tried to run away

from their lives. The birds didn't
care, except the downy woodpecker,
who, it appeared, had something more

in mind, trying to drill himself
down to the elm's clogged heart.
It's not that I could just imagine

hearing him, like a miner alive under
the hand of the mine's timbers,
but more what I knew I was in

store for. Once, out walking, I saw
the shell of an elm in front of me
and how, in one step, I would catch

up with my tree-life, cursed and
blessed into a trunk and branches
the downy woodpecker would drum on,

until either the elm hummed, or full
and still, and finally still myself,
he could hear my breath knock back.

# PEARL OF THE MOON

For three days I cried
the dry tears of worry.
And then I wept for a week
until I was floating
on my own pond of tears.

I saw cove lilies open
and close, and the loon
open the mouth of the pond
and disappear, only to rise
later in his sister's

hollow song. Each night
the moon cast more
of its pearls,
until the whole pearl
of the moon hung

like a song from my neck.
Old saw-whet owl would
*tu* from the woods
when he saw the moon
singing in the water.

Tears meant nothing to him
but more water in which
to see the moon's song.
When wind dragged in
the night clouds,

he tried to fly above them
to find the singing

necklace of the moon,
and almost died in the branch-
less forest of the clouds.

I cried for three days,
until the pond strung
all of my tears
for that saw-whet owl
to wear, too.

# MOON OF ANOTHER CHILDHOOD

The moon rises over the Green Mountains,
lighting night's stones, half-floating
in the winter graveyard of the garden.
I see the scattered squash seeds
as did Kelley, the gardener, frozen
beads of a fairy's broken necklace.
Bleached vines of snow peas
stick up from their small mounds,
and the pale skins of unpicked tomatoes
are almost a bloody paper. Evening
grosbeaks pick over all the fallen
sunflower heads, and from the window
of memory's room, I raise the garden
of childhood and hold it. White
and pink peonies opened along the side
of our house; purple phlox filled
the spaces between the set stones;
and the pansies, carefully and confused
on the whim of their stems, responded
to night's blue suburban breezes.
My father brought home flats
of flowers for Kelley to plant,
whose brogue floated up from the bog
of peat moss he mixed by hand.
I could not follow the lilt
of his words, as he watered the new
lawn, made room for the transplanted
bulbs. But now I know he was singing of home,
speaking in sounds that tried to mend
the ripped Irish earth. At dusk, he would
load his rakes and hand mower,

his sprinklers and roller onto the back
of his truck, and drive to the little
Ireland inside the city, to its warm
beer and baritones, its song,
from this side of the ocean,
of an undivided island.
No longer able to afford his work,
my father had to let him go. Yet
Kelley returned each week to tend
everything he had started in
the ground and raised, rising
as the seed of this moon rises,
casting its green light over the halved-
pods and broken rinds, over the dug-
out bed of three-eyed potatoes.

# THE SLAUGHTERS OF FORT MATANZAS

Everyone has walked here or will
have waited for the ten seat power-
boat to take them across the blood-
less water. The boat's "captain"
retired from the refineries of New

Jersey, when he became used to seeing
oil burn the surface of the sea,
hearing children scream their delight
at the burning water. Crossing
the Matanzas River, no one can see

blood falling from the walls of the fort
or off the grasses growing over the un-
remitting French bodies. Anybody
would think they are taking a free
ride to a ruin and the letters

MATANZAS mean nothing anymore.
When a people name an unsuspecting
ground after its atrocity,
they can't be sure if its spoken
and written repetition helps

them forget or remember. Here
the sun reflects as far as a mile
off the windows of Summerhouse,
the nearest resort, and works
in the direction of forgetting.

And the unbandaged wings of the great
blue heron, the misfiring pistons

of the inboard motor and the unforgiving surf, each absorb the slightest sound which sounds like slaughter.

# SLOW WORDS FOR SHOREHAM
# AND THE APPLE BLOSSOM DERBY

All the runners and near-runners start
to stretch the night before, to push against
the nearest wall in their sleep, then bend over
clasping the back of their calves like swanning
ballerinas. Here in Shoreham's apple country,
the annual spring run begins again in the May
blossom of their minds. Back inside the year
these local running friends see the year go

off across a chalked-in starting line that starts
in a church parking lot and runs the falling
hills nearly five miles down to Lake Champlain
and the reversing Ticonderoga ferry. The race
organizers try to time the run to coincide
with when the millionth apple blossom breaks
open and the route is a safe paradise from
pollinating bees. History tells them the first

hill is the quiet killer, a quarter down
and three quarters up to the Revolutionary
cemetery overlooking the unblistered lake.
But then, as it is said at the marathon in mother
Boston, after Heartbreak Hill, it's all downhill
from there. In between the untimed meadows,
the saintly, dumbfounded Holstein cows each
year come more and more to look like Woody

Jackson's mindful paintings of them.
Down across the temporary finish line
to the only stone building nearby the water

holding its share of lead shot and blood—
which still runs over these bursting apple hills—
they run by and stop to remember who,
out of breath, shoeless and unnumbered,
lay down and finished before them.

# BETWEEN US

FOR MY FATHER

Although the Coliseum needs to be repainted
and fresh sawdust raked into the landing pits,
next year the Olympics take place near you.
The weather is more certain and half
the local people speak two languages.
You say you won't go. I stayed home, too,
four years ago, preferring the translated
images and slow-motion replays on the cold screen,
when the skaters and skiers raced at Lake Placid,
a place I can almost see from my bedroom window.
There are so many reasons not to be there
in person—the expense, the crowds, the inter-
national cafeteria where we must hunt to find
a menu we can understand. When you were young
you were fast and, unlike me, you could throw
and take a punch, a difference, I'm afraid,
that keeps coming between us. Once
away from home, hoping to understand
what you loved, I went to a prizefight
and was struck, moved, when the fans booed
an obvious mismatch, a kid, really,
being beaten up. Later they cheered
when equals bloodied and broke each other,
embracing when they were done. All I saw
was blood and, moving closer to the ropes,
real bruises swelling faster than ice could
slow them. Perhaps that was what I chose to see,
because I was alone in a strange city, surrounded
by men and women shouting in a different accent.
If we had been together or were to go next year

to the Olympic ring in Los Angeles
to see the fight for the gold medal, the raising
of the winner's flag, what difference
would it make seeing the young fighters
do this work for us?
We would still have to order food
in our own words, wait in line leaving the stadium,
and, when we reached home, explain
what took us so long and why we were embracing.

# THE PLACE WE NEVER WERE

The sky doesn't know who has been there,
even if a promise was made to it.
Father, you promised to take me back
to where I was born, when all there was
in front of us was a cloud of hope. Now,

hopefully, I won't put this air between us,
when we talk of how close we came to making
that trip. Whenever I go away, my son,
without saying so, promises to be there
when I get back. You've said the gin

rummy place you were stationed at when I was
born could have been anywhere. And going
any place together is a way to keep
a promise. Some soldiers you knew flew back
to the runway where they were born into the sky,

and others stayed away. I've always thought
that us not going was how you made me
practice flying by myself, and now think
you know if you returned, perhaps
the sky still could lift you far from me.

Anytime you want to fly from where you are
and meet me there, I might be that son
again, flying in, like the new phantom fighter
I never was, so low the turning radar dish
could not find me to scramble you into the air.

# BEYOND RESEMBLING

One mourner said how much you looked alike,
as if resembling your dead brother would be comforting.
My aunt said she could barely tell the difference.
You told me the hardest part of mourning

him was seeing all your boyhood friends again
fifty years later and sitting with your older
brothers, wondering whom death would touch next.
I sat between you and mother so I could be

closer to you. Seeing you cry, she whispered
you'd been bad like this for days. I couldn't see
anything bad or good, except your man's tears
saved up for fifty years, filling in the dry river

bed of your face. I wept, too, because that day
you were sitting next to me and we could weep
together, because I knew then in my life there was
nothing else I could do beyond resembling you.

# AWAY FROM ANY UNIFORM

During the war when I needed to cry
I would drive to the nearest airport
and watch the soldier sons and some

daughters come home or say good-bye.
In the common privacy of the terminal
they were free to weep in the company

of strangers. Before the war it took
going to a movie in which something went
wrong between a father and his son

for me to feel my throat tighten and my
eyes well up. The only time I saw my father
cry was when his father died; too much

had gone wrong between them for him
to want to fly back and bury that war.
I don't think the families minded me

watching or even knew their tears could
start mine flowing. In their eyes I was
another loved one waiting for his to come

back or leave. Now with us only half at war,
I've had to learn to cry away from any
uniform or family that isn't mine.

When a plane drones overhead trailing
the tearless smoke of its jet stream,
and my son looks up, who's seen enough

of war in play and on the news to know
some sons go away and die, I let him see
this tear he can take back to his wounded sky.

II

# AT THE DRIVE-IN BEER WINDOW

It began with a machine that could hand
us a ticket at a tollbooth, a bakery,
a delicatessen on the verge of failing.
But the machine that did it quicker called
in sick, and it would take a man and a man-
in-training, who would sometimes be a woman,
the better half of a week to unjam the thing
or order a new part which was delayed
on a shipping dock outside Cincinnati.
And when the part came it needed to be
installed with a new tool unimagined in
the mind of a college graduate hungover
since June. So we needed to have a Now
What invented. But because we didn't want
to leave the bedroom of our cars, someone
thought they could turn their store into
a window we could drive up to and exchange
valuables through. Imagine, in Georgia,
a retired farmer went so far as to
make a funeral home where friends and
relatives could drive by the former
teller's window and view their dead,
without ever turning off their engines
or having their respects heard, except through
the wire screen of the teller's speaker.
Except we don't have to imagine this. Out of work,
driving around, it's become the thing to do,
cruising for the shortest line where, if we
stall out or run dry, someone will open their
window to hand us a beer and push us to the side.

# FOR THE WOMAN AT THE FAST-FOOD FISH PLACE WHO CALLED ME PIG

In this place God leaves His morsels unguarded—
crumbs on the breadboard, an extra french fry
left on the cashier's counter, and now the colorful
and extravagant unlocked salad bar I not-so-

innocently graze, waiting for my take-out fish to cook.
Out of the corner of your eye, more than mother-like,
you notice my grazing—I think I am at home—
and turn your fork into a gavel, your raincoat into

a judge's robe. When I feel hungry or guilty, guess
which one wins? My hand floats over the carrot sticks
and bacon bits to the innocent croutons. I know
this franchise boasts nationally its charcoal-broiled

techniques, but the flames I feel are dragon flames,
spewing over me from your unslain booth. Beyond the
    rhyme,
I'm conscious my snitching *is* uncouth, my hand so
unsanitary you wish the plastic sneeze guard would crash

like a guillotine. The last broccoli spear I take
is the straw that calls your army out, in full chain mail,
visors down, shields up. You march to the teenage
assistant manager and report my deeds by amount

and appetizing category. Handing over my fish and fries,
he looks to me for some assurance that her eyes

will not find a sin of his for condemnation. Seeing
he does not choose or is too young to reprimand

my public cheating, she turns to me and, in a whisper
louder than one God found in His big way to turn
Adam out, she brands me Pig, and sits back down,
with all her ruling knives and forks intact.

# SPEAKING OF US

In the commercial for beer we are
drawn as a cross-section of all our
jobs—hard and soft hatters, men and
old-timers, blacks and women, white

newcomers—each putting in a good
day's work, so it seems we have earned
our Bud. As if the day adds up to one
unopened blossom from the beer tree

standing as a fountain in the fermenting
grainyards of America. In St. Louis the scent
of brewing hops drifts over East St. Louis'
endless unbottled ghetto which breathes

in the free fermented air. The Clydesdale,
a horse bred beyond strength and beauty,
freshly groomed and teamed, has become
our working picture of pleasure, as if we needed

a show plow horse from Scotland to draw us in
toward the unemployable night. When people have
nothing paid to do, we pay for it in places
and words like *ghetto,* another stolen team

of letters that has never been able to
contain our horror and all the unredeemable
empties, scattering as the bruised and beautiful
litter of this place that blooms for us.

## ON PAGE TWO

When I want a good laugh or cry
I turn first to the human
interest stories. A new editor
assembles them above the weather
and statements of circulation.
In my small town, the touching
and strange hide in front of me.
I count on these three or four
sentences each day, sketches really
of what happened to somebody.
Recently my "favorite" describes
the fate of a widower building
a hobbyhorse for his grandson.
He said he didn't know why he let
his mind wander or where to, but
he did, and ripped the fingers
off his left hand with a power saw.
His dog lying under the work bench
swallowed his thumb and soon after
was forced to throw up for a surgeon
who sewed it and all the others on,
which up to now have taken.
God or the whale spit Jonah back.
If it wasn't for the warm transport
in the belly of the dog;
If it wasn't for the dog instead
of his wife; If it wasn't for his
wife who wasn't there; If it wasn't
for the way his mind wandered
as he cut out the pine head
of the pony . . . I wouldn't want

that editor's job choosing what
to put in, what to leave out,
having to take home all the un-
printed laughing and crying.

# AT THE AUTO-TELLER

The drive-in shines like broad daylight.
Every ten seconds a camera keeps whatever's
there in front of it, mostly the same eye
of empty street, a drunk holding the paper
bag of his body by its wrinkled neck.
A month ago, sad and high myself, needing
more money to keep being alone, I fed
my plastic card into the "your" slot.
A slip came back that read *Don't leave.*
I thought I was dreaming or too buzzed
to know better, that the camera had caught me
for a local version of "Now You're On."
I pressed the cold buttons with my code again
and another slip emerged, half-printed,
half-handwritten, that called me
by my first name and said, *Gary, I mean it.*
I left and in the meantime got straight
so I could go back with more courage.
A few nights later I typed in the letters
of my password, and the you replied
on a receipt, *Where have you been?*
Like a boy, I tried to stick in the tips
of my fingers, to see if there was something
else behind the words, and felt what I thought
was breath. Every night since,
I've returned to wait for another
message. All I can do, it seems, is be there.
All I can do now is tell you *I mean it.*
*Don't leave.*

# THE HOTEL OF PERSONAL EFFECTS

This is no one's birth bed,
although it can be said
someone was born here
and became carried away.
On route and laying over,
a salesman sells himself
to his rented sheets. The pine
desk holds no familiar picture
of graduation's caps and gowns,
locating the graduates once
and for all, arm in arm,
in the happy darkness
of their robes. In its black
cradle, the phone
rings for an answer;
the overflow in the bath
accepts its fate, when a bather,
called to the phone, steps out.
The small chandelier
gradually dims, by slowly
turning the dimming switch,
and the room becomes a space,
the manager claims, for functions.
In the top drawer of the night-
stand, tonight's couple place
their personal effects, tomorrow
the young maid will find
and take home to put away
and look at later. Still, after
making love, they are led by
the imprints on the threadbare rug,

almost a path, to the glass doors
opening onto the balcony.
From there they see the outline
of the city's park, the street-
lamps and benches, the bouquet
of oaks and generous fountain,
the people of this place voted
to keep lit and bubble all night,
so a stray dog could wet her tongue
and those staring out,
away from home, shine naked
in the moving light.

# WAITING AT THE OFFICE OF MAGRITTE

Drawing in the smoke, looking at his painting
of a pipe, I stare and start to blanken,
as if a watch were being swung before my eyes

or someone sat behind me listening to my dream.
The letters underneath say THIS IS NOT A PIPE
and mean what they say, although

their aromatic fumes can fill a room
after the smoker leaves, the small fire
in his bowl extinguished.

When I look beyond the frame, the pipe,
hanging and unhung, floats on the wall
with his diplomas. A breeze gestures

in the smoke sifting through the screens,
and lifts the worried papers on his nurse's desk.
They flutter and land. Dozing, I dream

the great tobacco leaves cure inside
their sheds. Outside the young plants cool
under the field veils, staged to keep the crop

from burning, before it is cut and hung to dry
in the perfect room of its aging. Below
in the dirt cellar, a printing press stamps out

the Surgeon General's warning
CAN BE . . . CAN BE . . . and I barely hear
the three syllables of my name as I am called

into his clinic. Breathing out, I lose
the little death each breath holds.
Now my smoke is an S, now the body of a violin.

# THE TWO-HUNDRED-POUND
POTATO CHIP

When I put my hand in the wax
bag, often I pick out myself.

Wishing for something light and small
to go with a bottle of beer,

garnish the edge of my plate,
at this weight, I am the plate,

the table, a chip off . . .
my father said, Maine's pride.

Vocationally speaking, I gave up
the thought of undercover work,

too much night duty and always
having to look like you aren't there,

wearing what they wear, using
their ridged and salty accent,

walking a safe number of steps behind.
If I had my choice, I would settle

at the bottom of the local library
working my way through the oversized

and M's. But you know the rules,
no eating in the stacks, no talking,

there where my first order
of business is always to check out

who's skimming her text, twirling
her hair, blasé in the face

of the printed page. Who, after
the last technical phrase,

is beginning to feel that little
edge of hunger, one or two chips

could ease, let alone what
a handful could erase.

# THE HAND OF PEACE

In the fifties, on the first early morning
talk show hosted by Dave Garroway, who has since
died by his own hand, the Kellogg company
sponsored a contest for cats and dogs
their owners claimed could talk. A panel
of judges, speech therapists and lexicographers,
listened to the howls and whines, the growling
barks and meows, and judged which sounds
were closest to human speech. Each pet
spent a minute making the most of his voice,
and his master was paid increasing amounts
for any noise that turned into a syllable
and then a word. A boxer from Indian-
apolis, loyal to her time, sang the name
*Eisenhower* so well the General himself
invited her to the White House and later
took the dog on his campaign. Across
the country, pet owners were mouthing two
and three syllable words in front of their pets,
except the parakeet and myna bird, disqualified
because of their skill to mimic real talk.
A Vermonter thought of bringing in
a Canada goose that kept flying over her
in the nineteen fifties, who flew in a flock
that looked more like a tuning fork than a V.
Each time he honked he barked the words
*Look. Look.* Even if she could have
caught him, it's unclear how he would
have done sitting on the spot under
those hot studio lights. Dave Garroway sat
there for twenty years and signed off

each show with his hand held up
Indian-style, which today, flying over,
the geese still look for as a sign of *Peace.*

# HAVING WATCHED
# THE DAY AFTER

Half the nation watched the end
of the world on television, as if
the country could watch and then crawl
back to a natural night's sleep.
Before air time the big worry was who
would sponsor this broadcast, whether
children of a certain age should be kept
from watching, not be alone, and have
someone to talk with afterwards.
Seeing Lawrence, Kansas incinerated,
we were to think of our hometowns,
and when the mother of the farm family
kept making beds as the silos nearby
puked out their warheads, we were to
recall our mothers leveling
fresh sheets and blankets. A few
weeks after the blast with everyone
puking and losing their hair,
we could have imagined they were being
treated for cancer and that, too,
would have been true. Afterwards,
when the docu-drama ghostwriters thought
they had made us feel too much,
government and ex–government officials
were brought out to cool down
what we witnessed, by explaining their
theory of peace through strength.
All our lives in this Age, we have heard
someone else's version of our lives.
If we let them, they would have felt

for us, as the screen faded to
the Late News and the hour grew later.
If we had thought to, instead of watching,
we could have joined our other halves
in the next room, who stayed up reading
another few pages and writing letters
they would mail in the morning.

III

# ARRIVING

with the streetlamps recently
restored
a sweet hiss of gas
streaming into their globes
the lamplighter tilting his pole
to the glowing pilots

with the townspeople in doorways
at the lips of their windows

with their children after dinner
kicking a broken ball
through the evening
air

with the town dogs barking or asleep
near their overflowing bowls
of scraps

with the words of this place still
unknown
although a few had learned some
necessary phrases before
arriving
and can distinguish among
gestures
now they are here

with the town park empty
except for night and night's
commissions

with the stars of happiness
ticking
in the far flesh
of memories
they will commit

# ANOTHER TIME

FOR RICHARD JACKSON

If home is where the hills are,
then here in Chattanooga, you have
heart for us all. I live between
the Green and Adirondack mountains,
in a valley and near a lake
named for Champlain, but when I go
out to run, it's all up and down.
Whenever I am away from home
and don't know anything about how
far things are or steep, a friend,
like you, will say, *The hills aren't bad.*
Looking from your study window
or driving them each day,
you imagine turning the hills
into another time, by running,
leaves the body to rely only
on its heart, which, even
at our age, isn't enough.
I say *heart* because it is
the word we both were raised
to say the same way, our r's
dumped overboard with all the tea
in Boston harbor. Where you live now,
you cannot say this without a neighbor
noticing and asking how you learned
to talk this way. I don't know
exactly, but probably
you were there, too, on Patriot's
Day, watching the runners
earn their marathon, hearing

John Kelley had made it again over
Heartbreak Hill, I know now is not
one but three hills, making them,
at that point in the race, more
like the peak of your Signal Mountain.
Just watching me go out and back,
taking the hills one by one,
and leaving them as they are,
you know what it is like.
When you sit alone with a piece
of level paper, the paper needs
you to take its pulse, to lean in,
so you can see its breath.
This is the breathing you feel,
when you hold your fingers
to the paper's wrist, and pressing closer,
breathe it back its life.

## THE TWO OF YOU

I don't have to tell you
when life begins or ends.

Even with your other children
sitting beside you, losing

the unnamed possibility
of this one feels almost

the same as going into one
of their rooms where they should be

asleep and finding no one there.
It's hard to know how to mourn

what was physical and mindful,
that came because of the two

of you, yet went for no single
reason. I still carry the memory

of not conceiving and tell you
not because I think it is

the same as your loss but because,
when you lose something, I find

myself for a moment lost with you.
I don't know how this will change

you or if you believe your newly
planted cranberry bush bears a child-

spirit on which the cedar waxwing
feeds. When she needs to, she

can carry a berry back for one
of her young to end the moment

of his hunger and you can watch
her circle from one mouth to another.

# THERE

It's been too many years since we lived in Buffalo
with the War, and even the past cannot recall
all it has forgotten. I remember someone wrote
a number on my wrist as we walked down
Elmwood Avenue toward a demonstration against
George Wallace, who hadn't been shot yet. He said
to call it when we got busted and by the way
he had good acid. Then I didn't know what he meant
by "acid" and was only beginning to know I
could use my body by putting it in a place
the government objected to. I don't want to make
myself seem innocent or radical. I wasn't.
I was scared and confused. But when a Buffalo Tactical
Policeman pushed us with his nightstick
to keep us neatly on a sidewalk outside
the Hilton where Wallace was freely speaking,
I felt my body stiffen and can still feel it
to this day. One of the phrases we heard in the sixties
and saw written with magic marker was NO MORE
BUSINESS AS USUAL. So much business now,
fifteen years later, takes place at the keyboard,
especially the soft clicking keyboard of
the painless computer on which, it is said,
we "punch in" a program that can start the movement
of canned goods or warheads impossible to call
back. Now, when I dial Information to try
and find you again, I hear the fast circuit
talk of a machine searching its made-mind
for the right combination of letters and numbers,
the code that means you still live someplace
familiar and can be reached when you are there.

## TO FAITH

Before I would leave home, my mother
would sew my name into each of my clothes.
If I lost a hat or shirt, it could be
returned. Or if I were lost, I could
look inside the collar of my jacket
and find the map of my two names,
follow the stitching she had sewn in
by hand. Yours, Faith, is the name we
each want, so when the wind is heavy,
we can breathe in its one syllable.
What is it like living by the quiet
instruction of that sound, when the world
says *Don't lose faith,* as if you could be
lost? And how often when you hear your name
spoken, see it written or have to write it
out yourself, do you want to slip out
from under that voice or pen?
Your mother knew all we need is one
name, our first, and anything else
we add on is for the love of someone else's
family or love, which is the other word
we call you.

# FORD'S POOL AT FAIR LANE

Clara and Henry swam here at the end
of a cool day, toweling off in front
of a fire, sitting with scotch and waters
on one of the heated marble benches
invented for this steamless place.
Every knob is brass, the wood a waxed
oak whose wavy grain can be read
without much trouble.
When the swimmers died and left
these grounds to the school at Dearborn,
the trustees filled in the indoor pool
with sand, capping it with half
a foot of concrete. As in some museums,
we are welcome to dine here as part
of the public, and are quietly watched
so we will not touch anything that is
not ours. Often in a room that isn't
mine, all I want to do is touch,
to put my hands where they don't belong.
I know we've said ahead of time
we won't take anything our fingers
are driven to. It's harder just to eat
and think we hear the swimmers swimming
through the sand and want to break
the concrete cap to let them out
than it would be to leave empty-handed
and drive to some thin and rented room
where no one is watching and take
what we want to steal for free.

# HER APPREHENSION

Looking out this morning, I see
a doe feeding on the June grasses
in the back meadow. I call you
to join me, knowing
by the time you reach here,

she could disappear. Yet something
holds her until you come,
and we stand fixed in her apprehension.
It's not often, at this bright time
of day, a deer wanders out

of the woods. At dusk, the last
feathered light helps each emerge
and keep its distance.
Once, driving home late, I hit
a doe, crushing her rear legs.

She might have felt she was alone
or the fast light safe enough
to cross through. When I tried
to move closer, to kill her quickly,
she dragged herself across the road

and down into the darkness of a lake,
barking with all the bloody air
in her nose. She must have died
on her own, no matter how often
I dream of another night to drive home.

Today there is just wind and field
between me and this new doe, and now

you still near, watching
her browse the shining trefoil,
the clovers' purple headlights.

## IN JANUARY EVERYTHING
## THAT CAN BREAK
## BREAKS DOWN

The small engines of our life
together quit.
When I try and draw water
from the tap and nothing
happens and you flip
a switch only to engage
the knowledge of what
you take for granted,
we look at each other
and say, *In January*
*everything that can break*
*breaks down.*
Janus bore two faces
to see his wife
both ways and sat
unadorned at the door
of heaven with no switch
to turn on or off.
Here, in our broken
heaven, I don't think
there hums a machine
of ours we couldn't
live without. Today
when all our two-faced
machines break down
and each repairman
we call is out until
next year, I think we
can make things work

if, as they say,
we put our heads to-
gether. First rather,
let's start repairing
where we turn our faces
in to touch. Let's crank
the little horsepower
from our lips.

# IF YOU ASKED

I can't say for sure she and I won't
touch, that a few bars from a song
hanging in the air might not be
enough to change what we thought
into what we did. That sounds too

country and western, but sometimes
those young bar singers saw what
they sang sitting night after night
in front of them and had to say it
outright to keep from taking it back

home to their rented room. I think
if I mouth their words, even when
we're kept close apart by the chords
of a slow dance, there still will be
time to think past what it might

feel like now. Thinking how I would feel
later is one way. Or what I would say
if you asked. I heard Hank Williams
had a bad back and sang from that pain,
too, as well as how he knew we get lost

when we touch and when we think not to.
He tied words to knot below the skin,
half because on hard nights he was strapped
into his guitar to keep him standing.
He knew what he had to lose.

I don't want to do anything to lose you,
even if you don't pick to ask. What I'm

not sure of yet is how to unsing a kiss
and, kissing you, strum out what I didn't
have the heart to do.

# MEETING IN MID-AIR

On the ground I learned
we nearly met. Fifty feet

of air between our planes
and no space on the air

controller's screen to keep
our green blips apart.

Thinking he thought we were
dead (I often think of death

through someone else's eyes),
lets me say, *I want to be*

*closer to you.* If this is
what it takes to say these

words, I hope I often have to
fly, and that the only thing

he sees on his night screen
is one plane and the wind

nearby for which there is no
neon sign. The only thought

I don't want him to think
is how, looking out

into the star-held sky,
with you not sitting here,

I need your hand to fly.

IV

# DANCING AT BREAD LOAF

## 1

Snow will drift over these porches,
and Cherry, Birch, and Maple,
dormitories of summer, write out
their shadows across the covered fields.
Yellow boards of the buildings
will appear gold against the snow.
If we watch from our August windows
while we stay here now,
we won't pass by in March,
mistaking this place for an abandoned inn.
At the Little Theater we will need
to pull off our gloves and scrape the frost
from a small pane, in order to see
the stacked and folded chairs, the empty stage.
By then the great hall will be
a closed heave in the wind, a cooling oven,
and the pond, frozen over, nowhere to be seen.
Skiers can draft their lines across
the drifting fields, breaking the surface
of the snow, their steady poling taking
them out of sight. The winter moon will fix
its stars from falling. But sitting out tonight
after the last reading and dance,
preparing to go back tomorrow to our separate
cities, we can see the ecstatic summer
stars, falling and erasing themselves
from this page of the universe.

2

At tonight's good-bye dance,
I turn into a husband and touch
you in the thin agreement of dancing.
Caring for yourself, you ask about my wife,
so we are a pair of three, touching
and not touching in the perfect pulse
of the electric bass, the wavering flow
of the steel guitar. Here the moon is
the mountain's eye and the white noise
of crickets the steady sound of overhearing.
When the music is over,
the borrowed voice of the singer returned,
we are left alone to decide what to do
with our hands and lips.
Later, out in the star-chilled air,
the precise pins of stars hold the punctuated
sky, and I can look up and see her asleep
in our married, half-empty bed, turning
in the early morning dream of good-bye.


3

Between dances, sitting with you by the face
of this fire, looking through the amber eyes
of the owl andirons, I remember
the first time I came here, seventeen.
My father took the wrong turn off
Route 7, thinking this was the college
he wanted me to see. A brook running west,
going the wrong way, ran beside the road.

Writers rocked on the porches,
convalescing I thought, although the books
they held made this look more like a school.
None of them was remotely my age,
and the buildings named for the nearby
trees were unlikely dormitories.
I had no way to imagine myself staying,
and told my father to turn around
without stopping. He had the presence
of mind to stop and ask where we were.
Telling you, I still try and turn
one of them into Frost, who may have been
there or near enough so I can say he was.
A year later enrolled in the real college
in town, before classes began, I hiked
with the other freshmen to Frost's cabin.
Homesick and missing my city, I didn't see
his three apple trees giving their fruit
to the ground or the stone wall running
down the right side of the hay field.
I didn't hear the nuthatch and chickadee,
the underswell of crickets and breeze,
or feel darkness shining in the woods.
The first stars were giving themselves
away, and it was all I could do not to
go with them, now not to go with you.
Later that night at the student dance
in the Barn, I fell in love. Whenever
I return and meet you in this place
and we have not decided what our words mean
or where to take them, I can't tell
the difference between history and geography,
the difference between words that move me
or if you made them move across the night sky.

4

Once far from here, drifting over
the divided streets of my city, I
heard two trumpets and a saxophone,
a liquid lead guitar, a drum delivering
its pulse and a singer bending the blues
away from his listeners. I went in,
too scared not to, and stood listening
to the four-bar chorus.
Everyone there was black. I didn't
notice my mistake going in
was forgiven without asking for forgiveness.
Or that choosing, even by chance, to be alone
in the presence of others, a place by the bar
on which to stand. How easily I might
have been asked to leave or worse,
but that was only my thought, and no one
said anything except *good night* and *good-bye*.
I know there are places in your city
we aren't supposed to go, bars where we
could dance all night and forget our last names.
Here whenever I listen to music and want
to go one step further by dancing,
especially at the foot of this mountain
inside the Barn, I make sure I have brought
myself, and after the band gives away its songs,
out among the pulsing stars, you invite me
to go home to the comfort of my own loneliness.


5

Today with no readings or workshops to attend,
we could have taken a path into the woods

behind Frost's cabin and walked through
a cathedral of pines. Or the other way,
east, halfway up Worth Mountain, we might have
climbed to the abandoned ski jump and hiked
to the crater lake of Lake Pleiad
to swim, even with the rumor of leeches,
then slept out under a hiker's lean-to.
Across from the Inn beyond the mown
meadow, West-Running Brook goes
as Frost's poem says it does. If we had asked,
a caretaker would have given us keys to the Printer's
Cabin or Tea House. Both have stone fireplaces
and the ashes of their own stories.
Behind Treman there is a good sitting stone,
too large to have been moved by hand or team.
Sitting there we would have heard bumblebees
combing the farms of goldenrod around us,
and known how strange it is not to be noticed
this well. A half mile past Frothingham
through the stone gates on the left,
we could have found a field of blueberries.
Other couples have returned with full baskets
and traces of blueberry on their lips
and hands. Tonight sitting out, talking
about the places we might have gone,
we are bound to see the falling stars,
the constellation traced in the letters
of our first names.


6


Dozing at this dawn hour, you say
on rare occasions a bird is assigned
the name of the person who first saw it,

like Richardson's owl, the earless one.
The trees, cherry, birch, and maple,
carry their sound in the wind,
and, at first, have no other
meaning in our minds. When a mountain
suggests the perfect mystery of asking
nothing from us, we conceive it
in other terms, trying, the expression
goes, to bring it down to earth.
Here the mountains are no green mystery,
but in August the days bask in
themselves and the nights shiver.
Behind the Barn, past the pond,
that mountain disappears in the presence
of its mist, and appears to drift
off its mooring when the sun flaps
across the woods. After the last word
is spoken for this summer's conference,
staying up all night dancing and
following the stars,
we can enter the flour of dawn
and breathe in the scent of rising
bread, drifting down this distant morning
where, sleepless and falling
awake, we are still preparing to go.

V

## THE BOATHOUSE

O Kindheit, o entgleitende Vergleiche,
Wohin? Wohin?

O childhood, O images gliding from us
somewhere. But where? But where?

    Rilke (Jarrell trans.)


Here our Rhine is the White River,
sliding by like a slow cloud.
With only one memory between us—
once we watched the August stars row

themselves around the moon—
we must open the great overhead door
of the boathouse, letting out
what we each remember like rowing

shells slicing the summer water,
true and watery arrows.
Among the casual New Hampshire canoes,
you see yourself, a girl swimming

the Rhine again, reaching the male
and untouchable barges, grabbing
a connecting cable whose steel threads
still slice your mind and the red words

by which you remember. From this dock,
I see my father holding me over
the Niagara River, the falls green and gray,
the thought of him letting go—did he?—

still a dream which cannot stroke
me through the night. Out there,
a coxswain counts above the perfect
heave and pull of his boat, past

the pain his crew will forget.
How can we remember anything
when those bodies work like that,
one body stroked by one voice?

How can we remember who we, too, will be,
when all the canoes and shells are out
of the boathouse and we can walk in
among the empty racks and extra oars?

# FALLING AWAKE

When I was drowsy and they were
trying to put me to bed,
mother and father would fly
to the words of their childhood,
as if I had disappeared, and they
were alone in their room,
the door ajar, their syllables
of immigration
marrying them again. Sometimes
now, even when I am not

tired, feeling two puffs
of their familiar breeze,
*gai schlafen, gai schlafen,*
go to sleep, I begin falling,
today under the branches
of the box elder, a bluebird
has landed for the first time,
in among the thick leaves,
so hidden I am not sure
this jewel rests there.

How can I love what I cannot see,
what I was taught not to love
this much, as if it were the same
sex as me, our feathers ruffling
together? Where is the ribbed leaf
carrying the lovely word *faigeleh*
some use to mean *fag,*
mother first meant to say
*little bird,* perhaps bluebird,
perhaps this one?

# THE ACCENT OF THEIR VOICES

The map told its truth.
But when I finally lay
down on this short bed,
saw the moon come in
and heard the sea skip
a wave in its tide, I

thought (the way a night cloud
can split the moon) I was in
the wrong bed, the wrong house.
Without you here, the things
I thought were yours lost
your touch. I didn't know

whether to freeze and hope
to fall under a hand of grace
or rush out back into Maine's
summer darkness. Even the child-
star Goldilocks sat, ate, and slept
before she was discovered

and the moral to her story decided.
Upwind, I couldn't hope to give
my life to a stern and compassionate
bear, licking blueberry juice
from his claws. How many times
had I wanted to crawl into a bed

other than my own, first as a child,
only to recall the broken chair,
the bowl of porridge, how when

the lights approached and the door
opened, I thought I could make the growl
and accent of their voices mine?

# CAN I COME DOWN

I don't remember how many times
I was sent to my room. Too many?
Too few? But in Detroit when
a neighborhood had no other way
to cry or strike back, it broke all
its own glass and struck a match
no one could blow out. The mayor

tried to put everyone to bed early
by calling out the Guard, calling
up the moon. But they knew when
the real moon rose and didn't close
their eyes. I was stuck downtown
without a drink, all the bars
closed with the five o'clock streets.

Remember that ploy, shouting from
your room, *I need a drink. I didn't
get my kiss?* A cabbie said he'd drive
me across the river to another country
for a bottle, if I didn't tell
and would pay his price, guessing I
could pay the price for someone else.

That's when I thought I couldn't sleep
without a drink. There's no curfew
in Michigan tonight from what I know.
And I can stay up all night
drinking in the voice of the thin moon
I hear calling from its unlit room,
*Is it time yet? Can I come down?*

# POSITIVELY BLUE

FOR CAROL HOLLY AND ALVIN HANDELMAN


Seeing the name Delphi again
on the ruined map, this rainy morning,
I remember the blue day,
still without children,
we planned to lose ourselves
at the top of Parnassus
in the broken shell of Apollo's temple.
Four hours from Athens, slower than
the first marathon, beyond the plains
of melons and pistachios, up along
the sheep farms, the stone shepherd huts,
to one of the beginnings of the world,
the view repeats itself down to Itea.
Looking at sunlight waving the walls
of the mountain, the ancients said their god
was born here, and dressed a widow in garments
of a young girl, drugging her with smoke,
turning what she said into prophecy
and the right to lie down with her.
We walked through fumes of the idling
buses, and starting up the path to the ruins,
you told me to go on alone; you felt tired,
sick of traveling and spoiled food.
Walking by pieces of sanctuaries and shops,
I saw the stories of battles and games
struck from the split rock. Up in the sacred
precinct of Apollo, the sun leapt out
of my head, and all sadness of conceiving no
children left for the moment of that mountain.
Later, in the cool museum, I saw the Charioteer

in his bronze robes, holding the empty reins
in his remaining hand, his chariot and four
horses escaped somewhere between us. He held
the solitary stare of statues which says
*I'm here inside,* hypnotized more by the loss
of his team than his death or the metal cast
to my staring. When we met by the bus,
you were still sick, and driving back,
every so often, a wave of sickness passed
through you and then over me. It stayed past
Delphi and the next months, until we returned
home to the rain and the result that this time,
when we tried, turned the laboratory's child-
treated paper positively blue.

## PRAYER FOR MY SON
## ASLEEP WITH HIS SWORD

Now is your time for swords,
knives, daggers, a sharp word

and, this year, a bright cosmic
lightsaber called THE FORCE.

When you cry out
in your sleep, I come in

and pull up the covers you've kicked
off. You must feel something

change, because you smile under
the sleep of your eyes

and reach behind you to find
the plastic handle of your knife.

There will always be a sword
sticking in a stone, looking for

its true name, waiting to be
wakened from its cold dream.

Yours, Sam, is another word
for Arthur and the syllables

I see on your lips that say
the Jedi name Luke Skywalker.

When the cold comes inside
your covers, may you hold

the hand of your dream.
When a stone stops singing

the story of its king,
may you lend it your sword.

When you roll over and feel
nothing beside you,

may all my mays
and THE FORCE BE WITH YOU.

# THE TWO OF US

Out walking, holding hands, you say,
*Look our shadows make an M.*
I wasn't thinking how we start

to write ourselves across the snow
until the sun changes or one
of us decides to let go. But for you

at three, the world beside our house
spells itself into alphabets
that start with A or M. I've been

meaning to show you how some things
work—the grosbeak's bill is forged
into a V in order to split a sunflower

seed, and the brook below our field
only looks like one because we've had
a January thaw. For a minute

I've forgotten you're not two
and not asking why all the time,
although I bless you now for how you've

made me look more closely, even at
a sparrow's nest near the roof's peak
which threatens to clog a vent

and will put me higher than I like
to climb on our extension ladder.
Letting go and running ahead, your

arms and legs fly through the letters
of the alphabet like a sailor flagging
through his semaphore. I do see some

of the words your red and blue snowsuit
spells and, when you fall, the shape
of the angel that lies there under you.

# USING THE AIR

When I approach, the nesting
killdeer half flies into her
life-saving act, forgetting herself.
Limping into the air above the broken
cornstalks, she means to distract me

from the mud and straw ground
of her young. Once, my son fell
from a branch of our box elder,
and not able to reach him
soon enough, I saw him hold

his breath in a death-scream.
I could not see anything else
among the spear-shaped leaves
except the sight of him
going blue. I could not breathe

for him the breath he needed
to let go, so air could fly
back into his small lungs,
blood rise to his face.
It's true, whenever he is out

of my sight now, I worry.
And when I come this close,
mother killdeer uses the air,
pretending she cannot fly,
and I believe her.

# AS MANY OF THEM AS WE COULD

The stones down to the sea look
like stairs, rising out of the crashing
foam or falling from the cliff edge
of someone's rented summer lawn.

A commemorating plaque says giants
used this way to step in and out
of Baily Island's roily surf.
On the verge of putting words together

our children believe what they see
in the brass letters, the gigantic
granite blocks. Having felt monsters
in the safe dark of their rooms,

they don't have to step down
to feel the water heave up its dream
gods here. When they are older
and can read by themselves the name

of this place, Giant's Staircase, they will
have taken their first steps away
from us, who walked out of the sea,
carrying as many of them as we could hold.

# INSIDE

*Daddy, did you know there's a real person*
*inside that monster?*


The eyes are the right size and shape,
the mouth in proportion. The jaw juts
because of an underbite, but who doesn't

have that in their family line?
It's easy not to notice the ears—
once covered by what passed as hair—

are missing, perhaps by accident or damaged
genes, and each hand keeps an extra
finger for symmetry. The stooped

shoulders lend the appearance of coming
in from the cold, and the shuffle
reminds us of Great-uncle John

who lived with a slow leg for most
of his life. The smooth horns curve
like handles on a trophy cup.

We accept them as we do birthmarks
or stuttering. The nails grow long
and retract like a cat's who learns

to trust us. Night is its neighborhood,
the moan of the river wind its song.
When it stays out all night,

there are fewer birds to wake us,
and the dogs return rabid.
Finally here, Incredo sleeps like

your brother home from college.
From time to time I take your hand
and we go back and look in, see

the real breath puffing out, the lines
across Incredo's face which say, even to you,
small one, when he sleeps, he dreams, too.

# FOR THE TEENAGE GIRL
# ASLEEP ON THE BEACH AT TRURO

You aren't the Christina
Andrew Wyeth saw and painted into a field
of canvas longing, looking from the grass
back toward her house, propped by her arm
like a foal whose legs could crumble.
Sunning in the sand with your oiled friend,
half-woman, you seem the perfect summer
love for any boy who could love
your crippled leg he will see later,
when you kneel and flap the day's happy
debris off your towel. I have wondered
how I would hold someone I loved,
if her body was twisted and I had
to see her in a beauty beyond what
her body offered. Would I stand
on the two legs of my heart I claim
anytime I go to the beach and listen
to the waves bringing themselves back,
anytime I look at all the lovely sea
trash and broken shells? Could I
let my bones and muscles carry me
to the tide's mouth, taught by the moon
to wash anything that comes as an offering?
Would I take what I was given,
what I had to give, forgiving myself
my own half-perfect body with which
I can lie down in this unpainted world?

# AWAY FROM US

When we say good-bye now,
it's most likely for good.

Not that we are dying, although
death, too, earns its diploma

and loves us as well as grand-
mother and grandfather. Today,

when we march in, we are still
held together by chalk dust

and the quickly scrawled
PLEASE SAVE. DO NOT ERASE.

I know I am not your father,
and yet as Roethke, another

teacher, wrote, "with no rights
in this matter," I say

these fathering words which will
take you further than you want

to go. I sense you want me to meet
your father, though we will have

nothing long to say. For him
to have shared you leaves us

speechless, wanting the list
of names and honors to go on

forever, because when you
march out, tassled and smiling tears,

you walk away from us both.

VI

# READING AT NIGHT

The words on this page
cannot raise the sound
of your voice until
I read them, silently
move my lips in the cadence
of their syllables.
When a breeze slips into
the room, it turns another
page, lifts a letter
on the night table, taking
your signature back
to the leafless elms.
My breath doesn't sound
like the wind, but sometimes

at night, when I step outside
of myself and lean down,
I hear the little air
escape like a breeze and slip
back into my paper body.
I need you to stand
over me then and move your lips,
until the words you are
reading revive the speechless
air and I can slide under
the one slow sound of your voice
back into the page
of my body.

# SUGAR AND SALT

Soon it was discovered some things
were not good for us. The more
we put our minds to it, the more

we found we could remove
without losing much of anything.
Craving familiarity, we learned

to replace what we had taken out
with things resembling the
original. Some bodies would not

be fooled. Records show those
who paid attention lived longer,
yet of the ignorant who ignored

warning, a few lived past their
lives, too. Science could not
foresee a pattern and history

told its story, a page of which
included us. We watched the goats
to see if we could find God near-

by. They drank the same water
we did and watched us to see
those streams we avoided.

Their bones were found beside
ours, as well as the sound
of a word we hadn't known how

to pronounce, we are beginning to
hear now, when the wind returns
what we had told it to take away.

# THE WAY OUT

*after Masaccio*


He sent His Angel to tell them,
hovering with a sword in her right hand,
pointing the way out with her left.

How did she know which way was *out*?

The painter, Masaccio, heard a wail
beginning in Eve's mouth,
and froze it in the gray surface
of this church's wall.

I come to pray her back
through God's gates, to lift
Adam's head out of his own hands.

I don't know what is worse,
being expelled or the judgment
they wear, realizing God chose
not to tell them Himself, although

anyone can see Him here
in the discipline of His Angel's
Wings, the wall's adherence
to Masaccio's darker paints.

In this chamber, he does not mean
for me, kneeling and looking up,
to escape the feeling, but rather to
take the hand of remorse and hold it
beyond what I thought I could stand,
until, rising and forgiven,
I can find my way out.

# LOCAL THEORY FOR OUR WORLD

FOR ROBERT PACK

When Berlioz scored in the kettle drums,
the Big Bang happened. Things that
hadn't mattered before mattered then.

But everything won in the first
second of creation we could lose now
in this century's thirty-minute war.

Sitting in your living room, listening
to music, carving shavings from a well-
aged cheese, we count our twenty

years of friendship with stories
of the pets that kept us held—pig, fox,
tortoise, and all the dogs given

back to the ground. Thinking of them gone
lets us think of dying. Conjuring the first
second of the universe lets us think

of what there was before things mattered.
We need to know that in order to begin.
Witches need thunder to stir

their spells, so Berlioz wrote thunder
into his drums. Even knowing his weather
is electronically expanded by the two

caves of your speakers, we still
stand and go to the night window to see
if the growling means a dog wants to come in,

or if the crack and roll says all Hell
has broken loose again and, with luck,
we are together when the world begins.

# HANDEL'S WATER MUSIC

What is called The River is
really the State Ditch,
dragged open in the twenties.

Now the real Seneca River
moves in a straighter line
over to Cross Lake.

The Iroquois used to stand
their weirs in the narrows,
trapping the melodious eels

who loved the darkness
of the reedy shallows.
Over there on the other

side of the Ditch,
what is left of an eel
husk sinks and rises

with any brave bone.
When he was hungry, Handel
cast out his broken nets.

The eel swam through
with the abundant bony sun-
fish, good for nothing else.

But the pickerel stayed
and the smallmouth bass
he lifted out, leaving

the water to swim in
the shiny scales
of the river.

# TO SNEEZE ON THE TRUTH

FOR VICTOR AND LOUISE REICHERT

In the Green Mountains, in the small, wordy town
of Ripton, a beloved rabbi from Cincinnati stays
in his gray summerhouse with green shutters at the edge
of the National Forest. He was a friend of Robert Frost
who lived a stone's throw away and slung the rhymed
     stones
of his slingshot, until the stars broke back into
their starry temple. In October, after the summer
people leave, the deacons of the Methodist church
ask this lovely Jew to call the Old Testament
out of the corners of their white frame church.
Like churchmice, we country Jews fill the pale
velvet pews with our remembering bodies and shiver
when his Hebrew words treat the air, Jesus,

from this room's cross, hears and remembers. The rabbi's
     first
words, a Boruch'hu, bless whatever needs to be blessed,
and what does not, the goldenrod, for instance,
by this time carried away by the combing bumblebees.
Before the first killing frost, the darkening flower-
heads fill our noses with this season's soulful air-
borne snuff. Itchy and warm in the storehouse
of our neighbor's God, we see our borrowed rabbi start
to sneeze and hear our grandfathers, who have paid
back the ground, say, where it says "In unison,"
Genossen auf di emes. Tonight, if this is where
the truthful stars come out, like pollinated words
that carry us away, we sneeze on them.

# WHAT TO FORGET

If their buds flower early, then the young
Macs swell too fast before falling,
before settling in the baskets of Jamaicans
we choose for the temperament of their soft hands.

If the bees fly out, gathering pollen
from clover and the newly crowning goldenrod,
then, in today's cloudiness, we predict
only a mild winter and start

extracting frame after frame of their reserves.
If August turns damp and the tomatoes
we failed to stake rot against the ground,
we blame ourselves and say,

*What else should we expect?*,
forgetting they can be picked and spread
on paper for the sun to ripen, or stored
in brown bags for darkness to do the same.

If frost is the mist that settles September,
we write notes to read later this year,
to remind us what it was like,
so we will remember next May

when we retrieve our rakes, open the strung
rows with the eyes of our seeds,
what, casting and covering again,
we need to plant and forget.

# BORNE AWAY

The nuthatch strikes something
   in the bald radial
tire hanging from the box
   elder. She may be one
of the birds who eats stones
   in order to grind the meat
of a sunflower seed.
   Or traveling upside down
she needs the extra gravel
   weight to tip her back
upright. All the grosbeaks
   in this corner of Cornwall
flock here. There never was
   one grosbeak anywhere
even at night. A pair of
   cardinals crown
the thawing ceiling of the ground.
   He could be the berry
his mate feeds on. Her beak
   drips a gone-by strawberry
red. The chickadees light
   like eighth notes,
sixteenths when a cat hunches
   behind the elder.
But when one doesn't see
   the shadow of this
morning's hanging goshawk,
   their feeding drops a beat,
and, hearing nothing where their
   own should be, in quick

conviction, simultaneously
they strike the safe ground
of the air and bear themselves
away.

# IT'S SOMETHING

when you can look out
and see all the spring field
grasses: calf-high alfalfa,

rye and broom—
and seeing hear Orin
Lowe's green patched-

together John Deere tractor,
asleep now in the barn, coughing
up the wavy July hill.

It's another thing
to gaze and smell the combusted
smoke combine with the yet-

to-be cut hay which will lie
down sweetly and be raked
into windrows for the wind

to dry before the baler boxes
and ties the field
into forty-pound boxes.

And to hear Orin say,
before he says it, he was
born in this blue clapboard house

and only his youngest boy
stays home on the farm,
who will weep when he snaps

another tine off the mower
on a field stone or runs
a fan belt down to its last thread.

So his father, unhooking a full
wagon, will stop and fail
at holding back from cursing

him and the hard green ground
which breaks all his sleeping
rebuilt engines.

# HOW WE KNOW WE'RE HERE

FOR CORNWALL IN CELEBRATION OF
THE TWO-HUNDREDTH TURNING OF HER TINE

When the fields are braided in wind-
rows and the cough of the kick baler
kicks another bale into the dry air

when apple blossoms bring the bees
out of the boxed cities of their hives
and the trees hum with their safe gathering

when rain washes a thin film of spray
from the apples' skins and the orchard
air sings and drones in the engine-strained
dives of the sprayer's deeds

when the sun edges the Green Mountains
and on the other side of day
the Adirondacks and all shades of known
light take place in the shimmer
and hay-scent of this mown valley

when elm, birch, and maple are signaled
again from something far and close inside
and signal us by turning each leaf on,
each leaf and pine needle back to the ground

when deer still run down between
the swamp and orchards and can be seen
before they are taken down or bound away

when first snow begins to fill in
the fields, turning a key in the town
shed that starts the powerful and pain-
ful happy heave of the town plow

when the lights blow and power lines
loop from pole to pole and outside
only the wind is speaking
in swirls, trying to get away from itself
in the smoky puff of a down-draft

when the snow settles and someone steps
out on the unbroken road on their skis
or newly tuned snow machine and sets
a track the next snow will erase

when the air barely warms enough
to draw the frost out and sap up
and the known mud of the road is tracked
into the added-on mud room

when finally the ground is bare and hard
enough not to break a shovel tip
we need to turn our Cornwall clay
back into useable earth

and digging down we hit the long store
of broken tractor pieces and bottle bits
clinging to the clay like burdock to a sock
and they are still held by some of our last names—

Abernathy, Robbins, Bingham, Sperry, Peet,
and Foote—to which we now add ours, turning
on the tine of our two-hundredth year.
It's how we know we're here.

# FIRST SPRING

"About Ten A Clocke we came into a deepe Valley full of Brush,
Wood-gaile and Long Grass, Through which we found little paths
or tracks and there we saw a deere and found springs of fresh
water of which we were heartily glad and sat us downe and
drunke our first new england water with as much delight as ever
we drunke drinks in all our lives—"

(November 16, 1620, Truro, Massachusetts)


They must have heard surf breaking the sand
into coast, and dry from drinking the left-over
dust of the ship's kegs, they went searching
for new water, tramping through the Cape's woods
toward the salty sound that carried them here.
Everywhere the blood-seeking mosquito bore
its small transfusion and the green-headed deerfly
branded the backs of their necks and arms.
How could they stay, not being blood-drinkers,
not having found yet and aged a fermentable fruit
into a fruit wine that could help them forget

and remember the beauty and loneliness of crossing,
of being here beautiful and alone? Thinking of freedom,
or rather a different pain, they risked going thirsty,
living on what they could find to take the place
of water. Rightfully, they thought of deer bending
to drink, trout that could not live in the sea.
And themselves, one dry day, stepping where they had
never been, not born here, but bound now to this
salt-free spring which could take their knees and hands
and lips, turning each of them into a body of water
through which the tearless Truro fish could swim.

## BEFORE NOW

Tonight a wren sleeps in the sanctum
of a pine bough, safe in its design.
When a wind breaks through the still
dream of the air, the wren's toes curl
to keep it from falling into the pile

of needles, fur, and bones below.
Never has a wren met the sleeping
ground at night, not even in a dream
that could carry it back to its branch
by dawn. By dawn each day's seeds have

spent themselves into the right
number of heartbeats it takes a night
to pass. One seed too few and the wren
must remember the taste of the pulp
inside the husk and, failing that,

the numerous striped memories
of halved shells. How far back the wren
must go to replace those seeds
becomes a task each day
for the historians of the sun,

who have begun their cold search
in the hope they will find,
in their shape and taste and sound,
a few seeds the wren can know
before now and when night falls.

# THE CONTEMPORARY POETRY SERIES
*Edited by Paul Zimmer*

# THE CONTEMPORARY POETRY SERIES
*Edited by Bin Ramke*

By the same author

*THE DAY WE STILL STAND HERE*     1983